EDGE BOOKS™

T0051051

PRO SPORTS
by the Numbers

PRO FOOTBALL
by the Numbers

by Todd Kortemeier

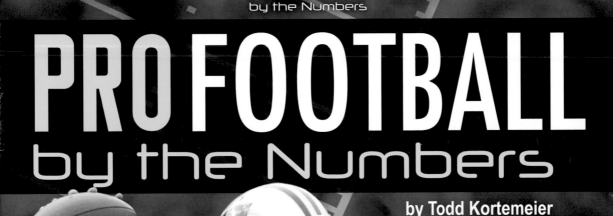

Consultant:
Barry Wilner, NFL Writer, The Associated Press

CAPSTONE PRESS
a capstone imprint

Edge Books are published by Capstone Press, 1710 Roe Crest Drive, North Mankato, Minnesota 56003
www.mycapstone.com

Library of Congress Cataloging-in-Publication Data
Cataloging-in-publication information is on file with the Library of Congress.

ISBN 978-1-4914-9060-0 (library binding)
ISBN 978-1-4914-9064-8 (paperback)
ISBN 978-1-4914-9068-6 (ebook PDF)

Editorial Credits
Patrick Donnelly, editor
Nikki Farinella, designer
Jake Nordby, production specialist

Photo Credits
AP Images: 15, Ben Liebenberg/NFL Photos, 5 (top), Bob Leverone, cover (bottom), 1 (foreground), Matt York, 24 (players), Michael Conroy, cover (top); Bettmann/Corbis, 5 (bottom); Newscom: Ai Wire Photo Service, 12 (top), John Harrell/UPI Photo Service, 12 (bottom), Patrick Schneider/KRT, 22, Rich Gabrielson/Icon Sportswire 252, 13 (bottom), Rich Graessle/Icon Sportswire CGV, 20; Owen Byrne CC2.0, 25 (bottom); Red Line Editorial, 17 (field), 19, 21 (bottom); Shutterstock Images: aceshot1, 20 (bottom right), Alexander Kaludov, cover (right), 26 (bottom), attaphong, 14–15 (top), B Calkins, 18, BEELDPHOTO, 24 (television), chrupka, 26–27, Danny E Hooks, 6–7 (background), 20–21, David Lee, 17 (silhouette), dean bertoncelj, 8–9, DeCe, 6–7 (foreground), 16, fzd.it, 26 (top), Gocili, 13 (top left), Henry Hazboun, 6, Joseph Sohm, 4–5, katatonia82, 24–25, kazoka, 23, LoopAll, 14–15 (bottom), martiapunts, 25 (top), Media Guru, 10, mj007, 20 (bottom left), mr.Timmi, 13 (top right), Nagel Photography, 17 (background), phoelix, cover (background), 1 (background), Robert Biedermann, 21 (top right), Spreadthesign, 9 (right), VitaminCo, 9 (left), vladmark, 12–13, 17 (middle), 21 (top left), 28–29; Theodor Horydczak/Library of Congress, 4

Design Elements
Red Line Editorial (infographics), Shutterstock Images (perspective background, player silhouettes)

Printed in the United States of America in Mankato, Minnesota
102015   2015CAP

TABLE OF CONTENTS

1970

Professional football traces its roots back to the 1800s in the United States. But for years the sport took a back seat to baseball, boxing, horse racing, and even college football in the battle for sports fans' attention. Then in 1970 the National Football League (NFL) completed its **merger** with the upstart American Football League (AFL). That move created the NFL we know today. The Super Bowl was a result of the merger. It also led to massive television contracts, new teams around the country, and many other exciting developments. These factors have helped make pro football the most popular sport in the United States. But it was a long path to get there.

Timeline: Milestone Years of Football

1912
The value of a touchdown increases from 5 points to 6.

1920
The American Professional Football Association (APFA) is formed.

1876
The first rules of American football are developed.

1906
The forward pass becomes legal.

1909
Field goals go from being worth 4 points to 3.

1892
William "Pudge" Heffelfinger earns $500 to play a single game, becoming the first professional football player.

1922
The APFA changes its name to the NFL.

merger: the act of making two businesses, teams, etc., into one
field goal: a scoring play worth 3 points in which the ball is kicked through two uprights

1960
The rival AFL begins play. The Houston Oilers win the league's first championship.

1932
The NFL's first-ever playoff game is played indoors at Chicago Stadium due to bad weather.

1966
The NFL and AFL announce plans to merge by 1970.

1970
The AFL and NFL merge into a 26-team league. *Monday Night Football* also premieres.

1967
The Green Bay Packers beat the Kansas City Chiefs 35–10 in the first Super Bowl.

THE GRIDIRON

In the NFL every inch of grass matters. It can mean the difference between a new set of downs or a drive-killing **punt**.

Penalties

Rules violations can prove costly. Teams can lose yardage when a player breaks a rule. How much ground is lost depends on the severity of the penalty.

$84.43
average price of an NFL ticket in 2014

$54.20
average Cleveland Browns ticket, cheapest in the NFL

$122.00
average New England Patriots ticket, most expensive in the NFL

5 YARDS
Common Violations: offsides, delay of game

10 YARDS
Common Violations: holding, offensive pass interference

15 YARDS
Common Violations: roughing the passer, unsportsmanlike conduct

SPOT FOUL
A spot foul happens when the offense gets the ball where a foul has occurred. Common Violation: defensive pass interference

punt: to drop the ball and kick it before it hits the ground

STADIUMS

1957
year that Lambeau Field, the NFL's oldest stadium, opened in Green Bay, Wisconsin

2016
year that U.S. Bank Stadium is scheduled to open in Minneapolis, Minnesota

82,500 capacity of MetLife Stadium, home of the New York Giants and Jets, largest stadium in the NFL

53,250 capacity of O.co Coliseum, home of the Oakland Raiders, smallest stadium in the NFL

100 YARDS length of the field

10 YARDS length of the end zones

53⅓ YARDS width of the field

99 YARDS

The longest pass completion has happened 13 times, most recently from Eli Manning to Victor Cruz of the New York Giants in 2011.

The longest run from the line of scrimmage was accomplished by Tony Dorsett of the Dallas Cowboys in 1983.

First-down rules: 4 downs to go 10 yards and get a new set of 4 downs

109 YARDS

The longest play in NFL history took place in 2007, when Antonio Cromartie of the San Diego Chargers returned a missed field goal. Cordarrelle Patterson of the Minnesota Vikings matched that distance in 2013 with a kickoff return.

end zone: the area of the field where touchdowns are scored
line of scrimmage: an imaginary line extending from the spot of the ball at the start of a play

THE PIGSKIN

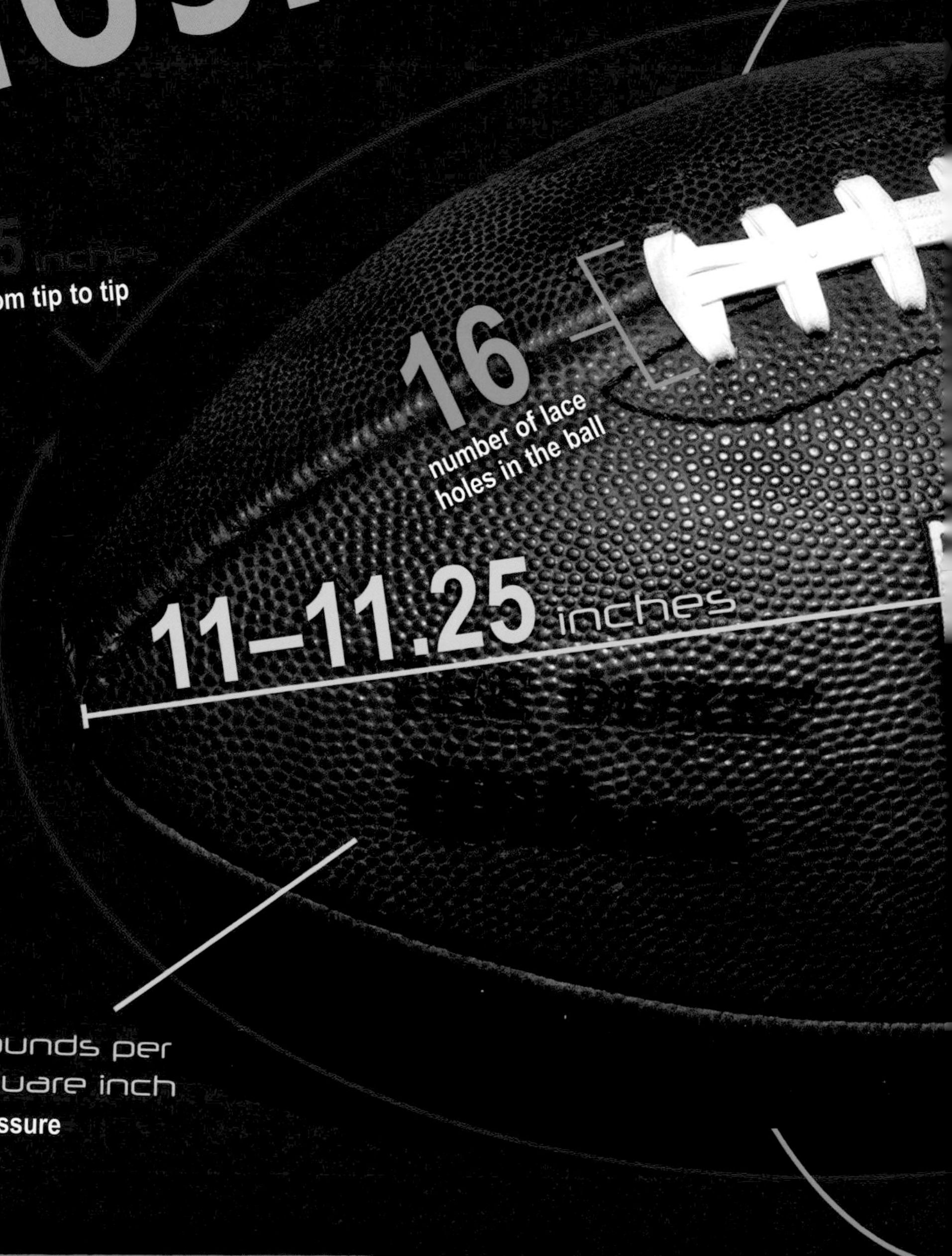

28–28.5 inches
circumference from tip to tip
and back

16
number of lace
holes in the ball

12
number of balls
each team
provides per game

11–11.25 inches

13 pounds per
square inch
inflated air pressure

circumference: the distance around something

The NFL ball has a unique shape. It is made to be thrown, caught, and carried. Though commonly known as the "pigskin," NFL balls are made from cow leather. Only one company supplies leather for NFL footballs—Wilson Sporting Goods. Here are some numbers about the ball at the center of NFL action.

700,000
number of balls that Wilson makes per year (less than 1 percent are NFL balls)

21–21.25 inches
circumference around the laces

108
number of balls that Wilson sends to each team every season

14–15 ounces
weight of the ball

8
number of balls for kicking and punting—called "K-balls"—provided by Wilson for each game

10
number of balls that can be made from a single cowhide

THE CHOSEN ONES
ALL ABOUT THE NFL DRAFT

Since the first NFL **Draft** in 1936, more than 10,000 players have been selected to join NFL teams. In the first year, only 81 players were drafted. By 2015 that annual number had risen to 256.

First-Round Draft Picks
(in the Seven-Round Era, 1994–2015)

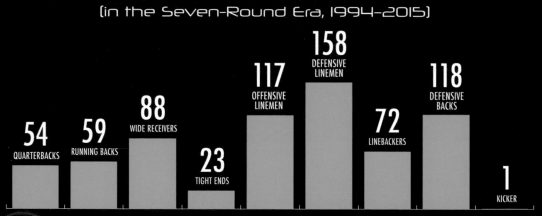

54 QUARTERBACKS
59 RUNNING BACKS
88 WIDE RECEIVERS
23 TIGHT ENDS
117 OFFENSIVE LINEMEN
158 DEFENSIVE LINEMEN
72 LINEBACKERS
118 DEFENSIVE BACKS
1 KICKER

PLAYER POSITION

THE COMBINE

Draft prospects undergo physical tests before the draft takes place. These tests take place at the NFL Combine, a meeting held every February in Indianapolis, Indiana. The tests show who can perform at the highest level.

45 inches
highest vertical jump
(Chris Conley, 2015)

4.24 seconds
fastest 40-yard dash time
(Chris Johnson, 2008)

12 feet **3** inches
longest broad jump
(Byron Jones, 2015)

draft: a process in which teams select eligible players to add to their rosters
tight end: a receiver who usually lines up close to the offensive line

linebacker: a defensive player who usually lines up behind the defensive linemen
defensive back: a player who primarily covers receivers and prevents them from catching passes

DRAFT HISTORY

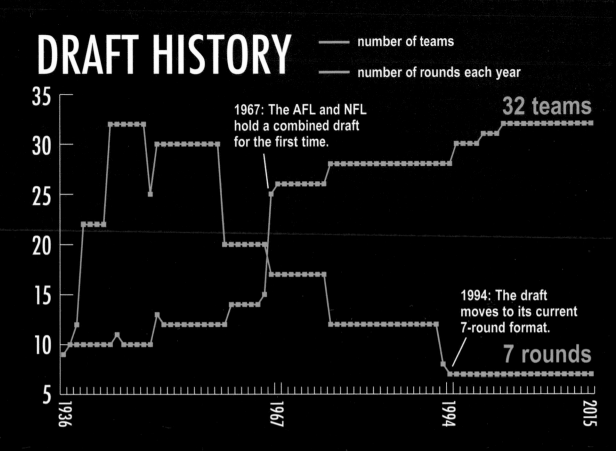

1967: The AFL and NFL hold a combined draft for the first time.

1994: The draft moves to its current 7-round format.

32 teams

7 rounds

35
30
25
20
15
10
5

1936   1967   1994   2015

Hall of Fame Picks

Pick 1 More quarterbacks (32) have been chosen first overall in the NFL Draft than any other position. Three of them are in the Hall of Fame. Quarterback Jameis Winston was the first player chosen in 2015.

Pick 74 Running back Curtis Martin is the lowest-drafted player in the Hall of Fame taken under the current seven-round format. Martin was the New England Patriots' third-round pick in 1995.

Pick 321 Offensive lineman Roosevelt Brown is the lowest-drafted player ever to make it into the Hall of Fame. The New York Giants chose him in round 27 of the 1953 draft.

15 Number of Hall of Famers who were not drafted but signed as free agents. The most recent was defensive tackle John Randle, who began his career with the Minnesota Vikings in 1990 and joined the Hall of Fame in 2010.

FIELD GENERALS

Quarterback is the most important position on an NFL field. But the quarterbacks of the past didn't play the same role they do today. Quarterbacks have always passed the ball. But they didn't pile up big numbers through the air right away. The quarterback with the most passing yards in a season is the NFL leader.

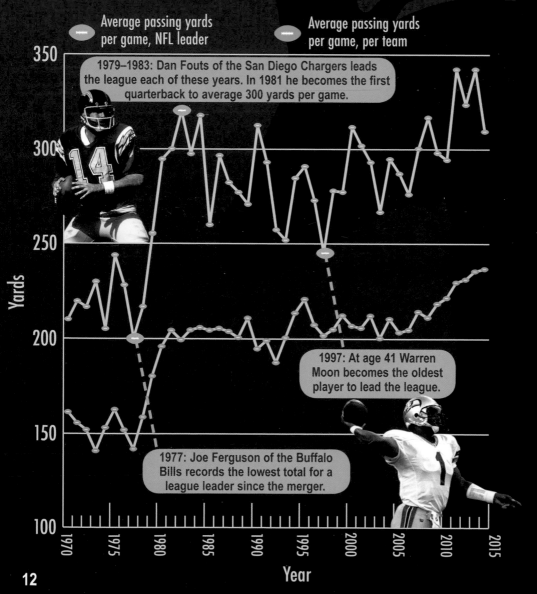

Average passing yards per game, NFL leader

Average passing yards per game, per team

1979–1983: Dan Fouts of the San Diego Chargers leads the league each of these years. In 1981 he becomes the first quarterback to average 300 yards per game.

1997: At age 41 Warren Moon becomes the oldest player to lead the league.

1977: Joe Ferguson of the Buffalo Bills records the lowest total for a league leader since the merger.

Yards

350

300

250

200

150

100

1970 1975 1980 1985 1990 1995 2000 2005 2010 2015

Year

ROUTE TREE

These are the nine basic routes that receivers run. Even-numbered routes break toward the middle of the field. Odd-numbered routes go to the sideline. These numbers are then used in play calling to designate the kind of route the play requires. Here is the route tree for a receiver lined up to the left of the quarterback.

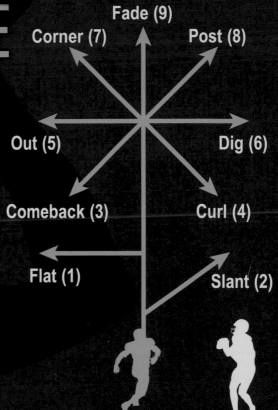

Fade (9)

Corner (7)   Post (8)

Out (5)   Dig (6)

Comeback (3)   Curl (4)

Flat (1)   Slant (2)

Career Leaders

Peyton Manning entered the 2015 season on the verge of holding the NFL record in three important career quarterback statistics.

Passing Yards

1. BRETT FAVRE, 71,838
2. PEYTON MANNING, 69,691
3. DAN MARINO, 61,361

Touchdowns

1. PEYTON MANNING, 530
2. BRETT FAVRE, 508
3. DAN MARINO, 420

Completions

1. BRETT FAVRE, 6,300
2. PEYTON MANNING, 5,927
3. DAN MARINO, 4,967

THE FROZEN TUNDRA

Football season starts in September and ends with the Super Bowl in early February. For teams that play outdoors, this often means dealing with bad weather. Snow is a common sight during games in northern cities. Cold temperatures, high wind gusts, fog, and heavy rain can also come into play.

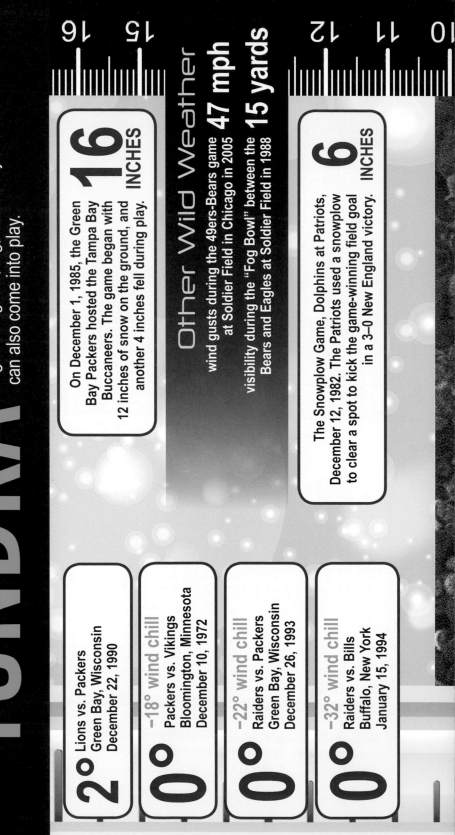

2° Lions vs. Packers
Green Bay, Wisconsin
December 22, 1990

0° −18° wind chill
Packers vs. Vikings
Bloomington, Minnesota
December 10, 1972

0° −22° wind chill
Raiders vs. Packers
Green Bay, Wisconsin
December 26, 1993

0° −32° wind chill
Raiders vs. Bills
Buffalo, New York
January 15, 1994

On December 1, 1985, the Green Bay Packers hosted the Tampa Bay Buccaneers. The game began with 12 inches of snow on the ground, and another 4 inches fell during play.   **16** INCHES

Other Wild Weather

47 mph wind gusts during the 49ers-Bears game at Soldier Field in Chicago in 2005

15 yards visibility during the "Fog Bowl" between the Bears and Eagles at Soldier Field in 1988

The Snowplow Game, Dolphins at Patriots, December 12, 1982. The Patriots used a snowplow to clear a spot to kick the game-winning field goal in a 3–0 New England victory.   **6** INCHES

The Packers beat the Cowboys in the game known as the Ice Bowl.

1.1 INCHES
Most snowfall on the day of the Super Bowl. The 2006 game was played indoors at Ford Field in Detroit.

0.5 INCHES
Amount of rain during Super Bowl XLI in Miami, Florida, the first rain to fall on a Super Bowl game.

-4°
−24° wind chill
Giants vs. Packers
Green Bay, Wisconsin
January 20, 2008

-5°
−36° wind chill
Raiders vs. Browns
Cleveland, Ohio
January 4, 1981

-6°
-15° wind chill
Colts vs. Chiefs
Kansas City, Missouri
January 7, 1996

-9°
−59° wind chill
The Freezer Bowl
Chargers vs. Bengals
Cincinnati, Ohio
January 10, 1982

-13°
−48° wind chill
The Ice Bowl
Cowboys vs. Packers
Green Bay, Wisconsin
December 31, 1967

GET YOUR KICKS

The kicking game may seem like an afterthought. It doesn't feature thrilling catches or big hits. But 3 points can often mean the difference between winning or losing a game, so having a great kicker is a must in the NFL.

64 yards (46-yard line)

longest field goal in NFL history, Matt Prater, Broncos December 8, 2013

61%

77.3%

90%

97.6%

100%

PERCENT OF FIELD GOALS MADE IN 2014 NFL SEASON

Seven points may seem like a guarantee when a team scores a touchdown. But the touchdown itself is only worth 6 points. Teams then must decide if they want to kick for one extra point or run a play for two. The single extra point has been more or less automatic, but the rules changed in 2015. Now teams that want to kick an extra point have to snap the ball from the 15-yard line, not the 2-yard line as it had been in the past.

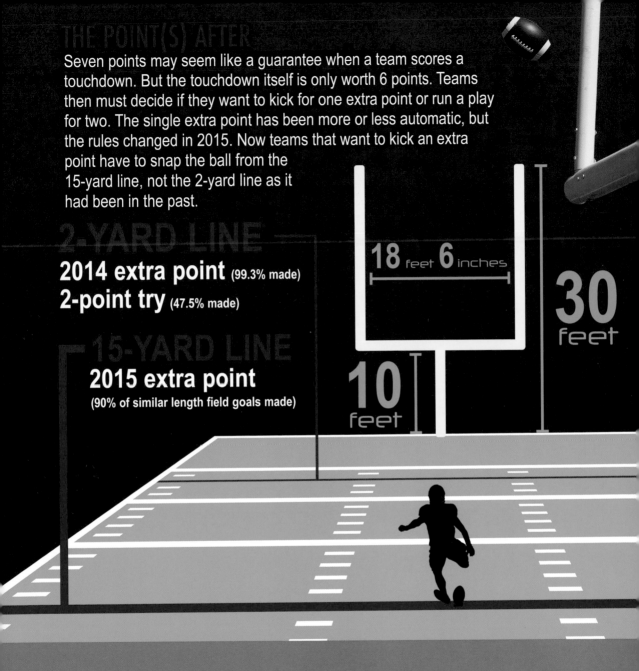

2-YARD LINE

2014 extra point (99.3% made)
2-point try (47.5% made)

15-YARD LINE

2015 extra point
(90% of similar length field goals made)

18 feet **6** inches

30 feet

10 feet

2-point chart

The following is a portion of a chart used by many coaches to help them decide when to kick an extra point and when to go for two. The strategy is determined by the time left in the game and the size of the team's lead or deficit.

LEAD BY	TRAIL BY
1: GO FOR 2	1: KICK
2: KICK (GO FOR 1)	2: GO FOR 2
3: KICK	3: KICK
4: GO FOR 2	4: KICK
5: GO FOR 2	5: GO FOR 2
6: KICK	6: KICK
7: KICK	7: KICK

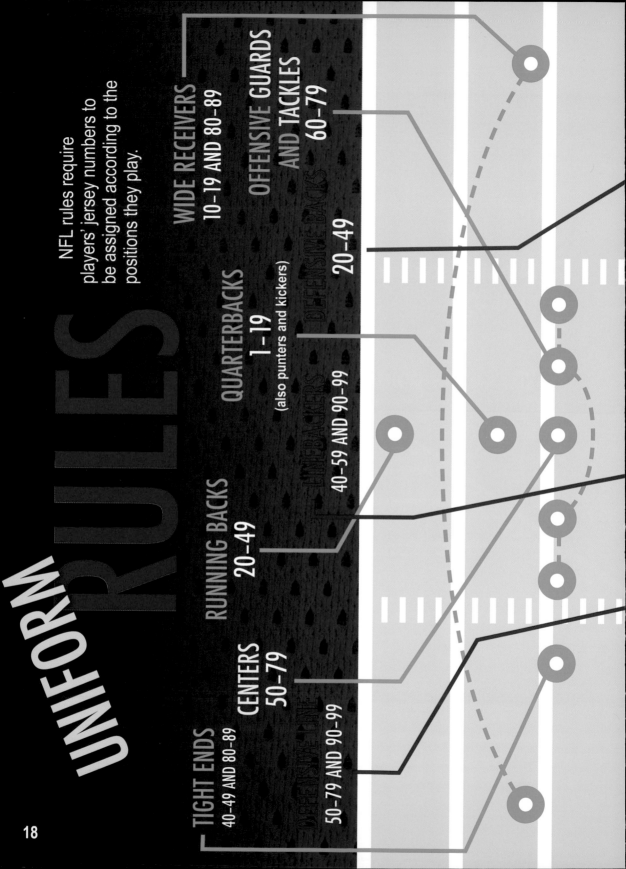

UNIFORM RULES

NFL rules require players' jersey numbers to be assigned according to the positions they play.

WIDE RECEIVERS
10–19 AND 80–89

OFFENSIVE GUARDS AND TACKLES
60–79

QUARTERBACKS
1–19
(also punters and kickers)

DEFENSIVE BACKS
20–49

RUNNING BACKS
20–49

LINEBACKERS
40–59 AND 90–99

CENTERS
50–79

TIGHT ENDS
40–49 AND 80–89

DEFENSIVE LINE
50–79 AND 90–99

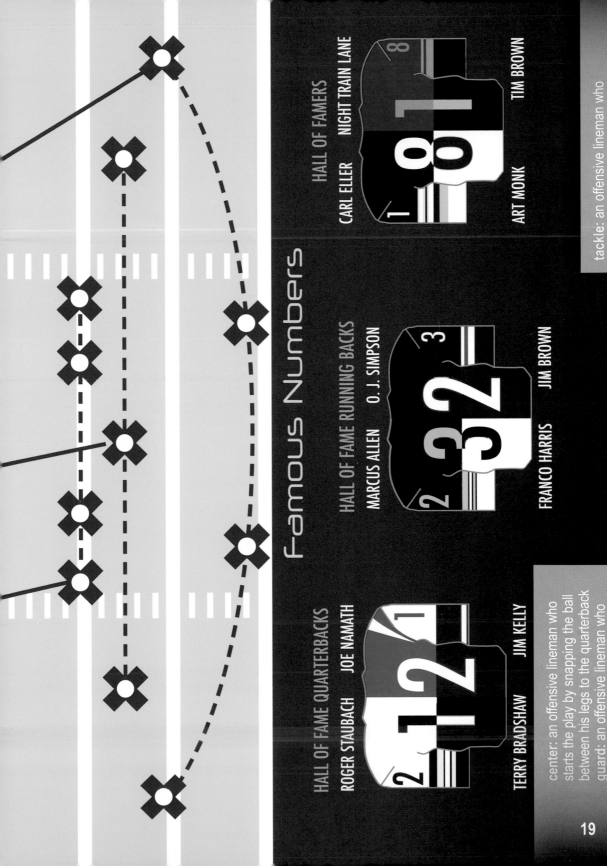

Famous Numbers

HALL OF FAME QUARTERBACKS

ROGER STAUBACH   JOE NAMATH

TERRY BRADSHAW   JIM KELLY

HALL OF FAME RUNNING BACKS

MARCUS ALLEN   O. J. SIMPSON

FRANCO HARRIS   JIM BROWN

HALL OF FAMERS

CARL ELLER   NIGHT TRAIN LANE

ART MONK   TIM BROWN

center: an offensive lineman who starts the play by snapping the ball between his legs to the quarterback

guard: an offensive lineman who stands on either side of the center

tackle: an offensive lineman who stands next to a guard

FOOTBALL BY THE 50s

50 Seasons

The NFL played 50 seasons (counting its first two as the APFA) before merging with the AFL.

1920

1/15/1967
First Super Bowl

1970
NFL/AFL
Merger

50 Super Bowls

Super Bowl 50: played on 2/7/2016

THE 50 YARD LINE

the line that divides one opponent's territory from the other; also where the coin toss takes place (and the chances of calling it right are 50/50!)

50 passing touchdowns

Only two players have thrown 50 touchdown passes in a season: Tom Brady (50) in 2007 and Peyton Manning (55) in 2013.

1950

the first year an NFL team had all its games televised (Los Angeles Rams)

Great players to wear

MIKE SINGLETARY
50
HALL OF FAME

KEN STRONG
50
HALL OF FAME

JEFF SIEMON
50
4 PRO BOWLS

MIKE VRABEL
50
4 SUPER BOWLS

PERFECTION VS.
NEAR PERFECTION

1972
MIAMI DOLPHINS

Regular season record	**14–0**
Playoff record	**3–0**
Super Bowl results	**WON 14–7**
Points scored per game	**27.5**
Points allowed per game	**12.2**

Close Calls
15–1 TEAMS

1984	1985
SAN FRANCISCO 49ERS	CHICAGO BEARS
(WON SUPER BOWL)	(WON SUPER BOWL)

The goal of every team is to win every game. But in the Super Bowl era, only two teams have finished the regular season undefeated. And only one of those finished it off with a Super Bowl win. Here's how they stack up against each other.

2007
NEW ENGLAND PATRIOTS

Regular season record	**16–0**
Playoff record	**2–1**
Super Bowl results	**LOST 17–14**
Points scored per game	**36.8**
Points allowed per game	**17.1**

1998
MINNESOTA VIKINGS
(LOST NFC CHAMPIONSHIP GAME)

2004
PITTSBURGH STEELERS
(LOST AFC CHAMPIONSHIP GAME)

2011
GREEN BAY PACKERS
(LOST IN SECOND ROUND)

23

SUPER BOWL
SUPERLATIVES

$4.5 million
cost to purchase a 30-second commercial airing during the game in 2015

114.4 million
TV viewers of Super Bowl XLIX in 2015

118.5 million
TV viewers of the Super Bowl XLIX halftime show

1,200 calories consumed by the average fan at a Super Bowl party

14,500 tons of chips eaten during Super Bowl parties

8 million pounds of guacamole eaten at Super Bowl parties

450 million chicken wings eaten on Super Bowl Sunday

13 teams that have never won a Super Bowl

6 Super Bowl wins for the Pittsburgh Steelers, the most ever

10 most times a city has hosted a Super Bowl (Miami and New Orleans)

8 times that a team has won two consecutive Super Bowls

4 teams that have not played in a Super Bowl (Browns, Lions, Texans, and Jaguars)

NO LONGER JUST "AMERICAN"

Pro football's roots can be found in other games played around the world. The NFL version is uniquely American, but the game is growing in popularity around the world. Most players still come from the United States, but take a look at how many players active in the 2014 season were born elsewhere.

Canada
7

Toronto
hosted six Buffalo Bills regular-season games from 2008–2013.

Haiti
3

U.S. Virgin Islands
1

Jamaica
3

American Samoa
3

Mexico City
hosted the first regular-season NFL game outside the United States (Cardinals vs. 49ers, October 2, 2005).

Tonga
1

29 American Samoa has sent 29 players to the NFL despite having a small population of approximately 55,000 people.

FOOTBALL

Estonia
1

Scotland
1

England
3

London
hosted 14 regular-season
games from 2007–2015.

Poland
1

Germany
10

Czech
Republic
1

South
Korea
1

Italy
1

Greece
1

Japan
1

Nigeria
2

Liberia
2

Cameroon
1

Angola
1

Australia
1

THE TV GAME

The NFL is one of the most-watched sports leagues in the world. NFL games are also among the most-watched programming on TV, period. The sport's biggest event, the Super Bowl, is frequently the most-watched television program of any kind of the year.

▶ TIMELINE OF THE NFL ON TV

○ 1939
The first NFL game is televised. But so few people have TV sets that only about 1,000 people in New York City are able to watch the game.

○ 1950
The Los Angeles Rams become the first team to broadcast all of its games, home and away.

○ 1951
The first national broadcast of an NFL Championship game airs on the Dumont Network, which paid $75,000 for the rights. The Rams beat the Cleveland Browns 24–17.

○ 1956
A Thanksgiving game is nationally televised for the first time.

SUPER BOWL VIEWERS SINCE 1990

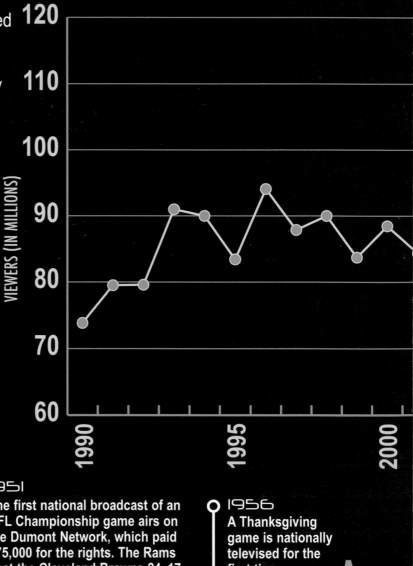

VIEWERS (IN MILLIONS)

$1 billion amount CBS, Fox, and NBC each pay the NFL per year for rights to air games

$2 billion amount ESPN pays the NFL per year to air *Monday Night Football*

$12 billion amount DirecTV will pay the NFL for 8 years to be the exclusive carrier of NFL Sunday Ticket, a satellite package that allows fans to watch out-of-market games

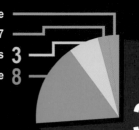

50 MOST-WATCHED SPORTING EVENTS OF 2014

College football title game
World Series Game 7
World Cup soccer games **3**
Winter Olympics coverage **8**

37 NFL games

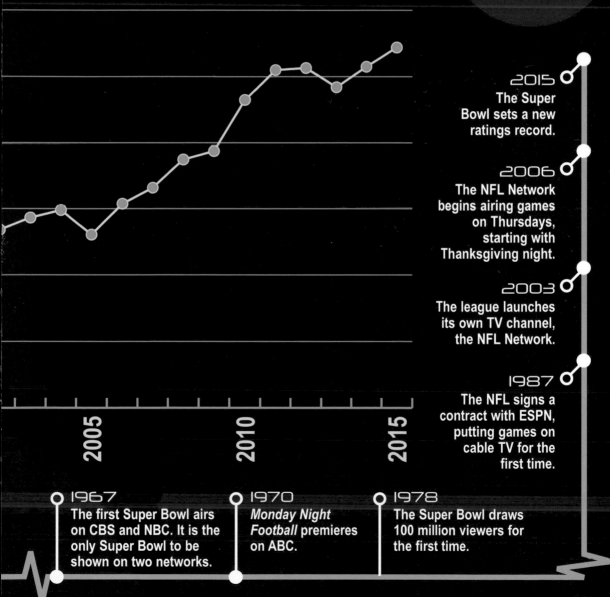

2005

2010

2015

2015
The Super Bowl sets a new ratings record.

2006
The NFL Network begins airing games on Thursdays, starting with Thanksgiving night.

2003
The league launches its own TV channel, the NFL Network.

1987
The NFL signs a contract with ESPN, putting games on cable TV for the first time.

1967
The first Super Bowl airs on CBS and NBC. It is the only Super Bowl to be shown on two networks.

1970
Monday Night Football premieres on ABC.

1978
The Super Bowl draws 100 million viewers for the first time.

Glossary

center (SEN-tur)—an offensive lineman who starts the play by snapping the ball between his legs to the quarterback

circumference (sur-KUHM-fur-uhnss)—the distance around something

defensive back (di-FEN-siv BAK)—a player who primarily covers receivers and prevents them from catching passes

draft (DRAFT)—a process in which teams select eligible players to add to their rosters

end zone (END ZOHN)—the area of the field where touchdowns are scored

field goal (FEELD GOHL)—a scoring play worth 3 points in which the ball is kicked through two uprights

guard (GARD)—an offensive lineman who stands on either side of the center

line of scrimmage (LINE UHV SKRIM-ij)—an imaginary line extending from the spot of the ball at the start of a play

linebacker (LINE-bak-ur)—a defensive player who usually lines up behind the defensive linemen

merger (MUR-jur)—the act of making two businesses, teams, etc., into one

punt (PUHNT)—to drop the ball and kick it before it hits the ground

tackle (TAK-uhl)—an offensive lineman who stands next to a guard

tight end (TITE END)—a receiver who usually lines up close to the offensive line